Cinders of My Better Angels

Cinders of My Better Angels

Poems by Michael Magee

MoonPath Press

Copyright 2011 © Michael Magee

Poetry
ISBN 978-1-936657-01-8

Cover photo by Peter Serko
Author photos by Peter Serko

Design by Tonya Namura
using Optima

MoonPath Press is dedicated to
publishing the best poets of
the U.S. Pacific Northwest

MoonPath Press
PO Box 1808
Kingston, Washington 98346

MoonPathPress@yahoo.com

http://MoonPathPress.com

Acknowledgments

The author gratefully thanks and acknowledges the publications in which some of the poems in this collection previously appeared:

The Arts for "Lifelines"

The Enigmatist for "Watching Olivier's Henry V During Chemo," "Sea Deep in Blue Ink," "Life on the Chemo Ward" and "Pet Scan"

In Tahoma's Shadow for "Icarus at Atlas"

The Jack Straw Anthology for "My Mother's Roses Learn to Praise"

Poetry for "The Hand"

Poetry Northwest for "Song For the Body Waking"

PoetsWest Literary Journal for "Melchoir," "The Moon Its Polished Self, Mother of Pearl Appears on Good Friday" and "My Father Appears in a Dream as Charlie Chaplin"

Pontoon for "Newton's Law"

Raven Chronicles for "Touched"

Real Change for "Pathogenesis" and "A Writer's Routine Physical"

To Jean, my better angel

Contents

I

Sea Deep in Blue Ink	7
A Writer's Routine Physical	8
Pet Scan	10
Newton's Law	11
My Flexible Sigmund Freudoscopy	13
Melchior	15
Cry Coyote	16
The Hand	17
Icarus At Atlas	18
Out Out Damned Sword	20

II

Icarus Risen	23
Performing CPR on Romeo	24
Lab Results	26
Consultation	27
Tumors	28
Admitting	29
The Orders of Chemo	30
Liturgy For A Colonoscopy	31
Watching Olivier's Henry V During Chemo	32
Song For The Body Waking	33

III

Lifelines	37
Eye of the Sparrow	38

Screen Test For Another Colonoscopy	39
Needle Exchange	40
Pathogenesis	41
Life On the Chemo Ward	43
Touched	45
Newly Minted	46
My Mother's Roses Learn to Praise	47
My Father Appears to Me in a Dream as Charlie Chaplin	48
The Moon Its Polished Self, Mother of Pearl Appears On Good Friday	49
About the Author	51

Cinders of My Better Angels

*Just say the report of my death
has been grossly exaggerated.*
—Mark Twain

I

I always find it more difficult to say the things I mean than the things I don't.
—W. Somerset Maugham

Sea Deep in Blue Ink

For now the white ministerial
moon keeps track—
all on accounting blue-lined paper
on the surface
under the goose-necked lamp
that precious ink that flows—
for it never sleeps on the
other side of its pillow—
watching instead from the top
of my window, opalescent cool
as a cat's collegial eye, staring in
so I do not stray under its observation.

Writing word for word some poem
of little note to anyone but me
for in its Confucian wisdom
it lets me be, not interfering
thinking I am amused in this cell
of my room, totally blinkered in
seeing only the wide dead sea
ahead of me, wave after wave
of blue line approaching—
as I try to see above it all, but sink
back and let its crest catch hold as
my iris floats on its little life raft
hoping for rescue to come along
in the shape of a period.

A Writer's Routine Physical

I am being examined
questions remain about my
sinus drainage and plumbing
post-partum blues
or my knee-jerk liberalism.

A scar travels along my leg
like Hadrian's Wall
which I tried to jump over and failed.
Routine sleep-disorder dogs me.
I need a wet nurse.

My cataracts are scraped clean
where lenses now float
like lily pads and my tinnitus
leaves my ears ringing
like a paranormal cell phone.

Bouts of old age mix with tonsillitis,
juvenile anger plagues me—
still my blood-pressure averages
highs and lows in Phoenix 130/85,
my temperature stuck at 97.6 FM.

In my temples I feel global
warming coming on, as glaciers
recede along my abdomen,
my nails grow into half-moons
like Tiki torches.

Finally my fossil fuel is running out,
the dipstick shows me quarts low.
I am ready to have my
odometer turned over, or trade
myself in for the latest model.

For the foreseeable future
I will be taking Metamucil and hoping
for jean therapy so that I will
fit into my future plans, getting
exercise by walking on my hands.

Pet Scan

Mark, the man from Louisiana
has a way with an I.V. track
injects the dye as I sit in a dark room
my veins coursing their tune
while I float along on a riverboat
going down river to New Orleans.

Where I'm taken for my MRI
laid out on a long white table
while Aaron Neville sings "Over You,"
Miles Davis' "Milestones" in my head.
As they roll the x-ray scanner over
my chest up and down like a barrel
I glow in the dark like a neon tetra.

With my x-rated tunnel vision
and the window of faux clouds above
I keep perfectly still, beating
time in my temples as they scan
my neck, arms thrown back over
my head like a starfish singing a chorus
of "Hallelujahs," a handful of "Amens!"

Newton's Law

I drink my barium milkshake
milky-white color
while I listen to a choir
of singers on a rock band station
some ongoing looping track
like the IV administered into
my veins that hums its radioactive
isotope orbit lighting me up like
a tracer bullet.

A never-ending U2 anthem
that plays while the barium
suffuses me with its icy smile
drinking in the banana-flavored
mixture through a straw bending
light as a pale Narcissus
knowing all bodies are in motion.

Newton's Law, we never rest
but rise in our atomic configurations.
No X-ray can truly interpret us
and the ground beneath our feet moves
like a ceaseless caterpillar.
Guitar riffs ripple through our skin
while sub-particles pulse.

O singer of our names, lab technician
who guides us onto the table where

we don our mortal robes, empty
our pockets of all valuables
while the scanner reads our genetic
codes, we lift our arms in hallelujahs
the needle jumps in the grooveyard
of the crowded house of the grave.

My Flexible Sigmund Freudoscopy

My Sigmoidoscopy wasn't that flexible.
I tensed up as the snake
                          went in.
If this was what Freud had in mind
when he I.D.'d the "ID," probing
with their camera like MI5
what were they looking for anyway?

Hidden canals in Venice?
As they discussed me like gondoliers
taking tourists for a ride decked-out
in another language of jargon.

My Sigmund Freudoscopy was something
like a bad not-so-subliminal dream,
"We're almost finished," they said.
And I imagined I was on the lagoon
coming back from the Lido

after going to a nude bathing beach
sand running between my toes
before I put my clothes on, putt-putting—

Safe back inside my dressing room
where I was dressed to the 9s
for Dinner at 8, promising not to return
dead or alive in my lifetime.

"Sang" or "Froid" this wasn't flexible
it was hard-core, soft-porn, half-corpse,
half-swan, more Zeus than beautiful Leda,

more rape by a psycho than analysis
trying to bite me in the end.

Melchior

I know you burn white sage
for me, in your backyard pyre,
that your heart often keeps
a log on the fire and that
you have made in your house
an arbor of red leaves over
the headboard of your bed.

As to sheltering our dreams
I also know how you
woo me with kind words.
I wish I had sacred beads
to give you, but your potion
of frankincense I rub into my skin
begin our journey once more.

You have made of me a believer,
the Gnostic texts of your
handwriting I keep near my head.
Come empty your urn, the jar
of your holy djinn, I will fill
with perfume from my tears,
make of you my sweet incense.

Cry Coyote

Somewhere during your dream
I felt your spirit leave
your body.

You made a little cry,
I felt you struggle, you made
whimpering sounds, coyote
was at my back.

I put my arm around your shoulder
to keep you from leaving, then
gently, after your moon-dance
fever was over

                      I pulled you back.

The Hand

    1

I watch the sun rise in my hand,
the rays break light between my fingertips
until sunshine fills my palm.
It stretches itself and yawns,
uncurling as the sun mounts higher,
extends those fingers spreading outward,
trembling before the heat of day.

And as the noon descends to dusk,
it marks the change and shivers.
Inside the thumb a crescent moon emerges
as darkness creases a closing palm.
And as the night secures its hold,
knuckles whiten, fingers clench,
and veins grow blue with cold.

    2

When the dawn came, my hand opened again,
but I was closed, and it had changed.
Veins stiffened like a mountain range,
rocky knuckles spiked the back country.
The fingers tightened to a fist;
the flesh raged on all day, all night.

Icarus at Atlas

*In memory of Charles "Chuck" McDonald,
truck driver killed in the Atlas Foundry Fire*

All at once I saw
a spark jump in the air
and I didn't come down.

Didn't come down the same
but in my eyes my iris lit up
like a green-eyed comet.

My hair on fire like sparklers
I might have crashed
in the middle of the freeway.

But when the propane tank
exploded I tried to escape
the heat wave propelling me

forward like a missile
until the impact made me roll.
I crawled down on my knees.

So fatally flawed it's true
I couldn't recover my legs again
no strings left for me to pull,

my skin in ashes, the rest
human wreckage while my
poor wings had turned to wax.

And everyone running away from
flames that couldn't fly fast enough
until I screamed from the fire—

for all those men who couldn't
hear, but found my body burned
into cinders of my better angels.

Out Out Damned Sword

Curled up in fetal position
my legs locked, I wait for
the biopsy needle, the sting
in my hip as the assistant
pats my leg, settles me
like a horse about to be put down.

They speak low, we talk
about Prague, the Old Town how
my Romanian doctor never liked
jazz until he heard it drinking
Pilsner beer in a sidewalk cafe
outside St. Vitus as I travel with
him along this path of pain.

The needle jumps along the groove
on my hip like it's on a record.
The jolt as it extracts bone from
marrow, burning heat born
in my blood, beads pop out along
my spine as the doctor calls to his nurses.
They commend my bones as strong.

As we rest for the second draw
I wait for the needle to bite.
They pat me down at my feet
under the blankets.
This time won't be as bad;
we're almost finished here, just
a little more to be sure it's out.
The sword of Damocles dances
                    over my head.

II

*Winter and Summer and the
topsy-turvy world of cancer.*
—Martin Blackman

Icarus Risen

I've seen Icarus—just today
sitting next to me on the bus
with his leather aviator's hat
dog-eared flaps, frizzed-out hair
his stitching has come undone.

All along his bomber jacket
barely holding his shoulders in
coming out at the seams, holes
in his hand-painted camouflage pants
stitched in sky-blue thread.

He's been grounded temporarily
sun-burnt face, rusty eyebrows
how far he must have fallen
just to get here, rickety warrior
of a God-like man, Icarus—

But he never seems to complain
with his bailing wire and patched
crash-course test-dummy smile
damaged arms hanging straight.

Maybe he's waiting for the next
incarnation, someone who will
fly him to the moon, attached
to his side like a booster rocket.

Performing CPR on "Romeo"

You were designated by our instructor: "Romeo."
Each of us tried to breathe new life
planting a kiss on rubbery lips
turning blue by now, more frog than prince
as one by one we blew our candle's
breath into your mouth,
a paraplegic dummy with no
arms or legs, placing a thumb
above your eye socket
like Yorick's skull, cupped
tipping back your head; then
drawing a finger along
your jaw bone, Tybalt's rapier.
We pinched you off at the nose
inhaling two long breaths
turned our heads to listen
for the signal of your rising chest
or the bells of Friar Lawrence.

Next, we traced across from your
underarms between the nipples
pressed clasping fingers into prayer,
we pushed the heels of our hands down
counting to 30 pounding on the crypt.
O tomb of your ribs, what a thumping
you took! We repeated again
a kiss for good measure, hoping
to resuscitate your truncated body,
hoping you wouldn't vomit forth
all the bile of the Montagues.
Instead, you sucked it up, waiting
for the kiss of death from a Capulet

which never came, just a line of
well-meaning students waiting
to get our first aid certificates
and good to go in your name.

Lab Results

She seems to know something
but says the tests aren't back yet
my blood work is fine, even though
it begins to drain from my face.
I congratulate my sentient self.

She says something about a home visit
which sounds like a death sentence
but maybe I'm reading into someone
else's life, besides for right now
I get my twenty dollar co-pay back.

Somewhere the meter is running
so I may as well write this poem
as they parse my skin cell specimens
the Gordian knot is tightening even now
as I roll up the sleeve on my shirt.

For right now I have a reprieve
and think about writing a treatise
about the metrics of scansion or
vice versa, my spondees relax
loosening up into healthy "I ams."

Consultation

Tonight the fear pounds at my temples.
I have heard the diagnosis: "Stage 4 Cancer.
I know this must be devastating to you,"
the doctor says. Once home, I turn it over

and look below my chest to see its bruise,
find swelling on both sides and think
that it has already begun, call emergency.
"I have lumps right now. I must be seen."

"These," my doctor says "are false alarms."
"There's nothing yet to worry about—no
lymph nodes here; go home and try to relax."

I trace the false ribs' recesses and puffiness
I guess has always been there, wait, dormant
for the body to bring me further news.

Tumors

They grow wiser inside me
where I can't see them, keep to themselves.
What's worse, they're worse than rumors
for no one spreads them or denies them.
They don't lie, but multiply of their own
volition with no encouragement from me.

False friends to an unwilling victim
if I could, I would starve them, but I'm
hungry. If I could I'd dry them up, but
I'm thirsty, so I harbor them hoping
one by one to shrink their mass killing
with the truth of chemo, not with kindness.

Admitting

People here today look lost. "I don't
care as long as they don't operate on me,"
someone says. The lobby is under construction
and no one can get through. The deli is under
the jackhammer's rule as people spin off
in different directions. It's Friday and we'll
soon be keeping each other company.

Here for leaky valves, or bones
that rattle, our heads are screwed on
loose; we look worse than "Schindler's List."
The unemployed, SSI, charity cases and elderly;
we are all here on life support, waiting
for hip replacements, or cataract surgery
and no one is admitting to anything.

The Orders of Chemo

A black nun in white habit
a heavyweight with white loafers
struggles to get up from the table.

And I in my white head scarf
by the unholy orders of chemo
wear my hair short.

Take the vows of physical
fatigue, some dizziness
and a hope for remission.

She stands to remind me
of her sacrifice, sister of mercy
while I sit like an ordained priest

in a brown upholstered chair
with my journal as missal
with orders not to drink.

I watch my weight, look
in the mirror to see if by turning
sideways I can disappear.

Liturgy for a Colonoscopy

My delicate bracelet I wear
eggshell white the printout of
my name and doctor's name
a keepsake, my birthdate too,
listening to "Waters of March"
as I wait for my turn
in the dark waiting room.

When called upon—
put on slippers and gown
one open in the back
one worn like a robe
to enter the dressing room
where I am led to meet
Amy, Arlissa and Sarah.

Leaving behind all traces
of my clothing disposed
in a white plastic bag
present my vein to the needle
and feel its jab, now entering
the Endoscopy with
its monitors and beeps where
they check my vital signs.

Then turn up the anesthetic
as I turn on my side
as though falling asleep
I close my eyes and lay me down
wanting to wake with
a clean slate, hoping the images
of my insides will be different
by the light of my grace.

Watching Olivier's Henry V During Chemo

As Henry the V
kisses Kate's lips
at Agincourt
the I.V. drips
France and England wed
their fingertips link
as I finish my "chemo"
the nurse removes the port
I hope for peace
that will end
with a happy kingdom
joined by blood.

Song for the Body Waking

Wake now, deep among pillows,
from the valleys of sheets, the folds of dreams where
 you slept,
from the rivers where you drifted without worry,
from the seven cliffs of care, and the lakes
beneath them, among the shallows of water and wind.

Let light pour from the breach, this slab of sky
now opening above your head. Stretch, feeling
all your length, the whole world
sprawling out before you at your knees,
this body where you begin.

III

*I watched the trees as they disappeared,
waving at me in despair and seeming to say,
"Whatever you fail to learn from us today
you will never learn."*
—Marcel Proust,
from *In the Shadow of Young Girls in Flower*
(translated by James Grieve)

Lifelines

> *When we try to pick out anything by itself,
> we find it hitched to everything else in the
> universe.* —John Muir

Picking up your feet, you may find the earth
wet and still clinging to your shoes beneath you,
a footprint as your sole signature.

Picking up a leaf, you may find the tracings
of your own green veins, fanning out, a lifeline
leading to the spider at the other end.

Picking up a rock may lead you to a history
of shadows from which you came, a white fossil
lightly pointing to your own remains.

Picking up your hands will lead you to fingers,
the opposable thumbs, your tensile grip, an index
of this tenuous world we try to grasp.

Like our lives, which we must never put down lightly,
knowing why it is we hold each other dear, attached
by unseen roots to this gravity we share.

Eye of the Sparrow

> *A sparrow does not fall in the wood without*
> *Him knowing it. His eye is on the sparrow.*
> *—Matthew 10:29, New International*
> *Living Translation Bible*

As I limp home
in autumn, I see my star falling,
but along the curb, I find sparrows
cleaning themselves digging little furrows
in the dirt among the leaves
appearing in twos and threes.

Skirting outside our coffee tables
they come to visit, always
on the lookout for crumbs, making
the most of what's around them,
they fill the holly bushes
with their song cycles.

I rejoice in the chatter of their daily lives
simple relief from the hawkers of news
purveyors and predators, while
the sparrows keep fussing around
and in their spirit I find good company.

Screen Test for Another Colonscopy

Today in the waiting room, a photo:
Fred Astaire, Ginger Rogers hoofing it
his knee bent impossibly back
at a 90 degree angle, she covering him
with a billowing starfish dress.

What angle will I take?
Prone to the world in my hospital
dressing gown, open at the back
while they explore my colon for tumors,
Cyndi Lauper's singing "True Colors."

In the lobby, they even have a small
screening room—here I imagine re-runs
when I look at the dailies it's not pretty.
I could use a top hat, walking stick
kicking up my patent leather shoes.

I trip the light fantastic while the camera
tracks me up the derrière, a dazzling
view in full-tinted grainy color stills
spectacular as Venus setting though
I could use another ending.

Needle Exchange

It's just the going in
pulling out that hurts.
I suck in my breath.

Feel the pinch in my arm.
"Ouch." The nurse winces
as though I've insulted her.

"It's nothing personal,"
I say. "I'm always this way."
And she flinches back.

"There, it's nothing you see!"
And I look away
trying to save face.

Pathogenesis

The ferry boats are made of white bone china,
sail in spirits across the water from Bremerton
past Alki and Duwamish Head, a drumbeat engine
thrumming in my head, safe port below silver clouds.
I sleep in my bed near Burlington Northern Railyard,
rolled up in my blanket like a cigarette,
the world made visible in smoke and wind—
vibrations sent along the line from another train's
        thunder.

Meanwhile, the feather of a gull
floats in the air above my skin, a girl on wings
calls my name, "Oh Santa Fe."
Your headlight burns a ring in my overcoat.
A leaf leaves color in the autumn air,
yellow words mingle with red paper from the
vine maple, the scroll of a madrona's parchment
as starlings scatter in the air like crosses.

"Oh, Santa Fe," the crow is cursing in the lines,
a cough comes from the throat of nearby woods
and robins nest in the masts of birches.
If I could find a way around this cold that thickens
like sugar in my blood, just for a cup of Joe
to hold against my chest, Oh Brother
would you spare some of your heart's wood
so I could live again, stir me with a breath.

Give voice to my fire, all along the ground.
I hear my belly's rumblings, my ears
echo like tin cans, a wire is strung tight
for me to hear, but there are only lullabies
from the railbeds where long lost children

once lived. I wake to the ashes of dawn.
What I wouldn't give to rub my eyes and find
pennies someone had put there just for luck.

Life on the Chemo Ward

Life is peaceful here, no pressures
among the beeping monitors,
the Benadryl has run its course.
My veins gently pulse smoke signals:
It's in the DNA. The D-N-A.

Linda has left with her go-pack.
I rest on my bed of laurels
drinking TreeTop apple juice, eating
cheese and crackers, Lorna Doones.
Only the occasional rhythmic tightening
of the blood pressure sleeve: *1-2-3.*

My heart is thumping its mantra
while I keep my Mona Lisa smile.
Life is my mistress in chemo-time.
I'm singing to myself as Nancy, my R.N.,
squeezes my hand: "You have the same
name as my son."

So far I'm doing *beautifully*.
I dream of banana milkshakes,
deviled eggs, clear chicken broth,
healing of my tumors, shrinking
around the horizon line
of my middle earth.

David with his hair loss looks
radiant as the Buddha.
We both have rare Lymphomas

a sign of divinity, perhaps.
We speak the same language:
Me, *Tonto* and he my *Kimosabe*
travelling the same chemo path.

Touched

She spoke to me first,
this woman who had medicine
the rib bone of a coyote,
the heart of a peacemaker.

She pulled from her red cloth
a Cherokee eagle feather,
brushed me on the face; then
closed my eyes and blessed me.

When I left I couldn't feel
my feet, my pulse was down,
my skin had been reborn
dusted by a waxen wing.

Filled with pure honey
of a hibernating bear
I walked tall as if I
had always been this brave.

Newly Minted

I look a bit like Roddy McDowell's
Caligula, my hair points to a widow's peak
or perhaps a thatched roof.
Silver garnishment of a feast
hair freshly mown on a new lawn
that is still re-seeding itself and will grow
again in a new estate, atop my
formerly bald pate.

My new eyebrow dormers
arch over my window panes
or sidebars telling a different story.
Someone said, "a lawyer or a senator,"
but I think George Clooney instead.
Or maybe I'm just trying to make a name
for myself that gives me a new cachet.

My Mother's Roses Learn to Praise

The roses on my mother's ceiling
open above me like Botticelli angels,
those pink, full-throated roses
my mother papered our ceiling with
like a garden, and I can hear her
playing the barrelhouse piano,
all those Scott Joplin rags raining down
like the "Maple Leaf" on our heads.

She's pumping those pedals even now,
shaking down the petals from our ceiling.
I can see them exploding full-out
into big-bosomed pink and red.
I can hear that ceiling calling to me
calling to my mother as she thumps
into her full-throttled heaven, pounding
out heartbeats into bass lines for the dead.

My Father Appears to Me in a Dream as Charlie Chaplin

Smiling, hair parted down the middle
he comes dancing to me from the mirror.
Head bobbing and winking, and twirling
his cane to cheer me with his silence.

As in slow-motion, he looks through me
ducking under and popping his umbrella,
and he grimaces a little as though
remembering the pain, but in this movie

his back is straight and when he bends
it's only a little creak, the smile
broadens, he makes a bow and pivots
to bring his face up close to mine.

The rouge brings color to my cheek,
until his hair is black and curly again
and when he tips his bowler hat this time,
it's nowhere near The End.

The Moon, its Polished Self, Mother of Pearl Appears on Good Friday

Is it a milky cataract
from my grandmother's long-ago eye,
the soft willingness watching me?

From a daybreak harvest
or a wide cat's eye that holds me
in its circle like a peerie?

It doesn't seem to blink,
but its open stare remembers something
you can't guess, perhaps a lake

where water in its vitreous aqua
lapped against a shore, but who can say
whether it's seeing in or out.

Leftover from last night when the
sky swallowed it whole, it opens its
polished self, appears as a pearl

on Good Friday and I am grateful
to the ever-giving sky that keeps making them
one by one. I never ask for more.

About the Author

From the echo of his grandfather's vaudeville patter to the sound of his mother's ragtime piano, Michael Magee's work has encompassed dance, theatre and photography projects, radio scripts, and a movie, "Shank's Mare." His poems have been choreographed for dance productions, performed as songs on the C.D. "Vaudeville," on-air for *PoetsWest* and as podcasts for Jack Straw Productions.

While in England, his play "A Night in Reading Gaol With Oscar Wilde" was produced. He also worked for Billy Smart's Circus in London and appeared on BBC radio, Nottingham and Derby. His chapbooks *Ireland's Eye* and *A Trip to Jerusalem* reflect his love of travel and trips to Italy, Czechoslovakia, Turkey and Morocco.

In 2010, along with photographer Peter Serko, Michael was co-curator and co-editor of *20/20: Tacoma in Images and Verse*. Three years of chemotherapy and ongoing cancer treatment have contributed to this collection. His prognosis for continued poetry is "good." He lives in Tacoma, Washington.

www.ingramcontent.com/pod-product-compliance
Lightning Source LLC
Chambersburg PA
CBHW032216040426
42449CB00005B/628